MATH POWER PACKS

Reproducible Homework Packets

Published by

Frank Schaffer Publications®

Columbus, Ohio

GW00888999

Frank Schaffer Publications®

Send all inquiries to:
Frank Schaffer Publications
8720 Orion Place
Columbus, Ohio 43240-2111

Math Power Packs—Grade K

ISBN 0-7682-3490-5

1 2 3 4 5 6 7 8 9 10 POH 12 11 10 09 08 07

Table of Contents

Dear Teacher,

We realize that extra homework practice is sometimes necessary for student success. *Math Power Packs* alleviate some of your heavy workload by providing ready-made homework packets right at your fingertips!

The packets in this book cover the six essential strands of mathematics—number and operations, measurement, algebra, geometry, data and probability, and problem solving—that are tested on standardized assessments. The packets were carefully crafted to meet national state standards and NCTM standards for school mathematics. To ensure that your students understand these important principles, a reproducible scoring rubric is included.

Each packet comes with a customizable cover letter to parents and ten activity sheets. All you have to do is fill in the appropriate information on the cover sheet for each packet, photocopy the reproducible pages, and send them home with your students. We recommend that you use these homework packets to reinforce the topics you are covering in the classroom. Send each packet home to give students further opportunities to practice skills, to help teach them responsibility, and to encourage independent work.

The home-school connection is an important one. To help strengthen and encourage rapport with your students' parents and guardians, we've included a blank calendar template. Use this to inform parents of homework due dates, upcoming quizzes and tests, and special events. There is an "additional notes to parents" section on each cover sheet that allows you to write specific notes and concerns home. You can also photocopy the math vocabulary sheet included in the book to send home so that parents fully understand the terms and concepts their children are practicing.

We trust that *Math Power Packs* will be a rewarding addition to your classroom. By utilizing the ready-made packets in this series, you are providing students with the extra learning power necessary for school success!

Sincerely,
Frank Schaffer Publications

Math Vocabulary List

centimeter—a unit used to measure length

circle—a closed round shape made up of points that are the same distance from a fixed center point

equal—having the same amount, value, or measure as another object

graph—a drawing that shows a relationship between two or more things

hexagon—a flat closed shape with six straight sides

how many are left—a phrase indicating that a student should subtract to find the answer

how many in all—a phrase indicating that a student should add to find the answer

inch—a unit used to measure length; equal to 2.54 centimeters

least—the smallest in size or amount

less than—a size that is smaller, or fewer, than another object's size

measure—to find the length, weight, or amount of an object

minute—a unit of time equal to 60 seconds

more than—a size that is greater than another object's size

most—the greatest in size or amount

number sentence—an equation, or statement, that shows a relationship between numbers

numeral—a symbol used to represent a number

octagon—a flat closed shape with eight straight sides

pair—two things that are alike

pattern—an arrangement of objects that is repeated again and again

pentagon—a flat closed shape with five straight sides

pictograph—a graph that uses pictures, instead of numbers, to represent objects

possible—capable of happening or being true. The opposite of possible is *impossible.*

rectangle—a flat closed shape with four straight sides, four right angles, and opposite parallel sides

set—a group of objects that are similar

square—a flat closed shape with four straight sides of equal length and four right angles

tally—to find the total of

triangle—a flat closed shape with three straight sides

Math Standards Scoring Rubric

1 = Does Not Meet   2 = Somewhat Meets   3 = Meets   4 = Somewhat Exceeds   5 = Exceeds

	Number and Operations
	Understands numbers, ways of representing numbers, relationships among numbers, and number systems.
	counts with understanding and recognizes "how many" in sets of objects
	uses multiple models to develop initial understandings of place value and the base-ten number system
	develops understanding of the relative position and magnitude of whole numbers and of ordinal and cardinal numbers and their connections
	develops a sense of whole numbers and represents and uses them in flexible ways, including relating, composing, and decomposing numbers
	connects number words and numerals to the quantities they represent, using various physical models and representations
	understands and represents commonly used fractions, such as $\frac{1}{4}$, $\frac{1}{3}$, and $\frac{1}{2}$
	Understands meanings of operations and how they relate to one another.
	understands various meanings of addition and subtraction of whole numbers and the relationship between the two operations
	understands the effects of adding and subtracting whole numbers
	understands situations that entail multiplication and division, such as equal groupings of objects and sharing equally
	Computes fluently and makes reasonable estimates.
	develops and uses strategies for whole-number computations, with a focus on addition and subtraction
	develops fluency with basic number combinations for addition and subtraction
	uses a variety of methods and tools to compute, including objects, mental computation, estimation, paper and pencil, and calculators
	Algebra
	Understands patterns, relations, and functions.
	sorts, classifies, and orders objects by size, number, and other properties
	recognizes, describes, and extends patterns, such as sequences of sounds and shapes or simple numeric patterns, and translates from one representation to another
	analyzes how both repeating and growing patterns are generated
	Represents and analyzes mathematical situations and structures using algebraic symbols.
	illustrates general principles and properties of operations, such as commutativity, using specific numbers
	uses concrete, pictorial, and verbal representations to develop an understanding of invented and conventional symbolic notations
	Uses mathematical models to represent and understand quantitative relationships.
	models situations that involve the addition and subtraction of whole numbers, using objects, pictures, and symbols
	Analyzes change in various contexts.
	describes qualitative change, such as a student's growing taller
	describes quantitative change, such as a student's growing two inches in one year

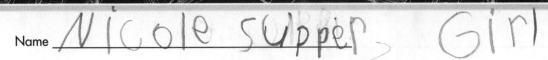

Name _Nicole supper Girl_

How Many Dots?

This domino has five dots in all.

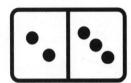

1. Write the numeral that shows the number of dots on the domino.

2. Draw dominoes that show five dots in all.

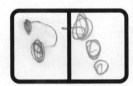 _5_

Write the number of dots.

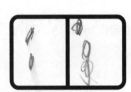 _5_

3. Draw dominoes that show six dots in all.

Write the number of dots.

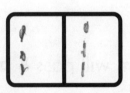 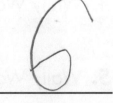

4. Draw dominoes that show seven dots in all.

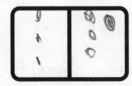 _7_

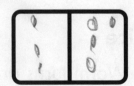 

Write the number of dots.

Name Nicole Supper Girl

Wally Worm

1 2 3 4 5 6 7 8 9 10 11 12 13 14 15 16 17 18 19 20

1. Which number will Wally Worm pass **first**? _____1_____

2. Which number will Wally Worm pass **last**? _____20_____

3. Wally Worm will pass 7 **after** _____6_____.

4. Wally Worm will pass 13 **after** _____12_____.

5. Wally Worm will pass 8 **before** _____9_____.

6. Wally Worm will pass 15 **before** _____16_____.

Power Practice

Wally Worm turns around and goes back. Say the numbers, in order, that he will pass on the way back. Write them down.

12
34
56
78
10
11 12
13 14

Math Power Packs: Reproducible Homework Packets *Grade K*

Name _____

On the Farm

Circle the correct answer.

I. There are **more** 🐖 than 🦆 🐔 🐄 .

2. There are **fewer** 🐎 than 🐑 🐐 🐄 .

3. There are the **same** number of 🐐 and 🐑 🦃 🦆 .

Seeing Spots

Circle yes or no.

1. More than 4 have spots.

2. Less than 4 have spots.

3. More than 1 have spots.

4. More than 2 have spots.

5. Less than 2 have spots.

Power Practice
How do you know your answers are right?

Something's Fishy

1. Color **more than** 2 fish brown.   **2.** Color **more than** 4 fish orange.

3. Color **less than** 4 fish blue.   **4.** Color **less than** 2 fish green.

Who Has More?

Circle the one that is **more**.

1. Lisa saw 5  .

Joe saw 7  .

2. Jada saw 4 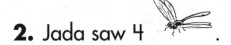 .

Alex saw 3 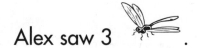 .

3. Dede has 12  .

Juan has 18 .

4. Jae has 8 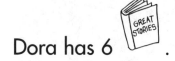 .

Dora has 6 .

5. Chae has 2 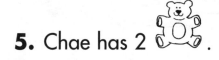 .

Tom has 5 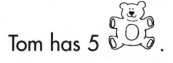 .

6. Aleta has 15 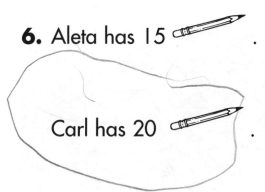 .

Carl has 20 .

Power Practice

 Tell a family member what **more** means.

Who Has Less?

Circle the one that is **less**.

1. Brent saw 3 .

Kida saw 5 .

2. Shaun saw 5  .

Lyn saw 8  .

3. Kris has 14 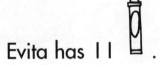 .

Evita has 11 .

4. Lili saw 6  .

Abby saw 9  .

5. Meg has 4 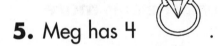 .

Tam has 7  .

6. Mark has 13 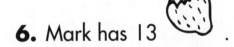 .

Paco has 16 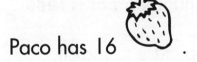 .

Power Practice

 Tell a family member what **less** means.

Show What You Know

1. Write a number. _____

Draw a picture to match.

2. Write a number that is **more**. _____

Draw a picture to match.

3. Write a number that is **less**. _____

Draw a picture to match.

In What Order?

1. Draw a line to match each penguin with its place.

5th   3rd   1st   6th   2nd   4th

2. The penguins changed places. Draw a line to match each penguin with its place now.

5th   3rd   1st   6th   2nd   4th

Power Practice

What happens if a penguin in the middle leaves the line?
What is the order now? Write your answer.

Numbers and Counting

Date Assigned: _____ Due Back to Class: _____

Parent's Signature: _____

Date: _____

Additional Notes for Parents:

Dear Parent:

This week we are focusing on numbers and counting. In the classroom, your child has been learning how to:

- •
- •
- •

The activity sheets included in this packet will help reinforce these skills. Please have your child complete the activity sheets by the assigned date, providing encouragement and assistance to your child whenever he or she needs it.

If you have any questions, please contact me at _____.

Sincerely,

_____

1–100 Chart

Point to each number as you say it aloud.

1	2	3	4	5	6	7	8	9	10
11	12	13	14	15	16	17	18	19	20
21	22	23	24	25	26	27	28	29	30
31	32	33	34	35	36	37	38	39	40
41	42	43	44	45	46	47	48	49	50
51	52	53	54	55	56	57	58	59	60
61	62	63	64	65	66	67	68	69	70
71	72	73	74	75	76	77	78	79	80
81	82	83	84	85	86	87	88	89	90
91	92	93	94	95	96	97	98	99	100

Name _____

Number Walk

The numbers below are scrambled. Put the numbers in order by drawing a line to connect them. The line has been started for you.

12	13	14	2 —3	
11	15	1	4	5
16	10	19	8	6
17	18	9	20	7

Power Practice

Where did you end? What number would come next?

Count the Animals

How Many?

Power Practice

Which animal does the farmer have the **most** of?

Count How Many

Color the dots. Count how many dots in each box. Write the number beside the box.

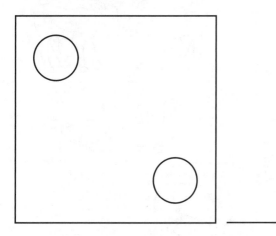 _____

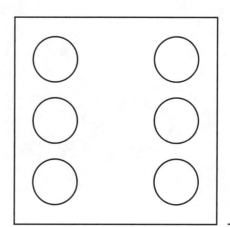 _____

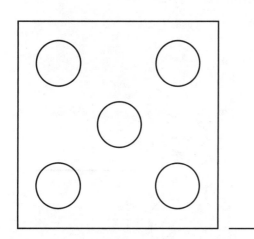 _____

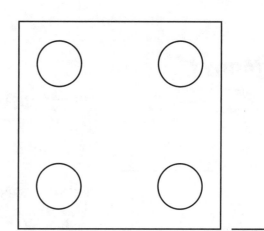 _____

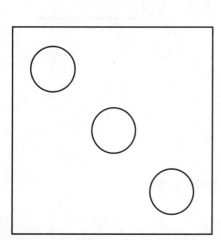 _____

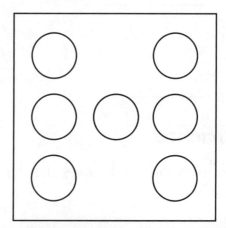 _____

Name _____

Count the Dots

Count the dots. Write the number.

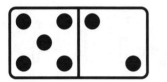 _____

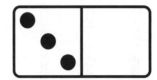 _____

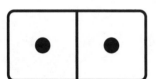 _____

 _____

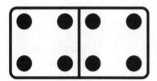 _____

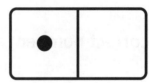 _____

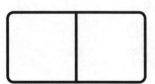 _____

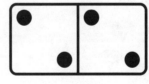 _____

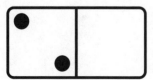 _____

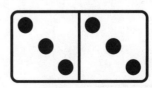 _____

Tool Time

Count the tools. Circle the correct number.

1.

2.

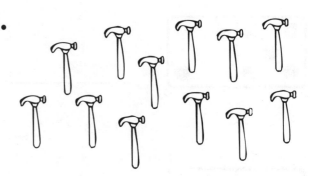

    9   **11**   **12**   **9**   **11**   **12**

Count. Write the correct number.

3.

4.

_____   _____

Picnic Time

Count. Write how many.

1. _____ 🐜 in the grass.　　**4.** _____ 🪰 on the food.

2. _____ 🐜 on the food.　　**5.** _____ 🪰 flying around.

3. _____ 🐜 **in all.**　　　**6.** _____ 🪰 **in all.**

7. How many bugs **in all**? _____

8. Write a number sentence. Show how many bugs.

_____ + _____ = _____

At the Game

Count. Write how many.

1. _____ boys playing .

2. _____ girls playing .

3. _____ children playing .

4. Write a number sentence. Show how many children **in all**.

Power Practice

What kind of math sign did you use in your number sentence?

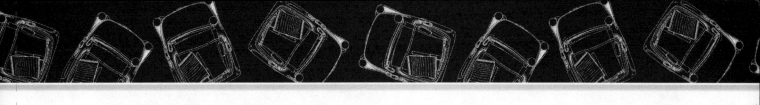

Count and Tally

Count how many. Tally in the boxes below.

How Many Are Left?

△ △ △ △ △ △ △ △

1. How many △ ? _____

2. Color 3 △ red. Color 2 △ blue.

3. How many △ are colored? _____

4. How many △ are **left**? _____

▢ ▢ ▢ ▢ ▢ ▢ ▢ ▢ ▢ ▢

5. How many ▢ ? _____

6. Color 4 ▢ yellow. Color 2 ▢ green.

7. How many ▢ are colored? _____

8. How many ▢ are **left**? _____

Power Practice

 How do you find the number **left**?

Number Facts and Operations

Date Assigned: _____ Due Back to Class: _____

Parent's Signature: _____

Date: _____

Additional Notes for Parents:

Dear Parent:

This week we are focusing on number facts and operations. In the classroom, your child has been learning how to:

-
-
-
-

The activity sheets included in this packet will help reinforce these skills. Please have your child complete the activity sheets by the assigned date, providing encouragement and assistance to your child whenever he or she needs it.

If you have any questions, please contact me at _____.

Sincerely,

_____

Fill in the Boxes

Look at the pictures. Write the numbers. Then, write how many in all.

1.

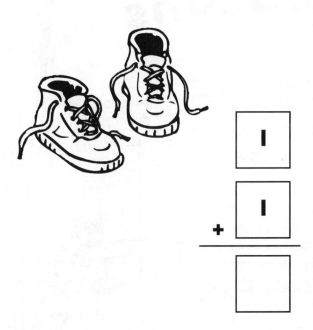

```
[ 1 ]
[ 1 ]
+
―――
[   ]
```

2.

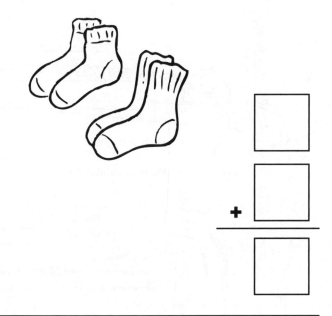

```
[   ]
[   ]
+
―――
[   ]
```

3.

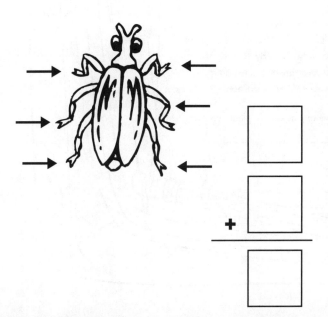

```
[   ]
[   ]
+
―――
[   ]
```

4.

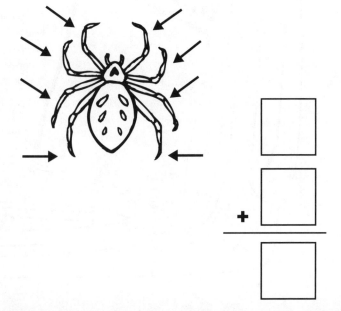

```
[   ]
[   ]
+
―――
[   ]
```

Double Dominoes

This domino is called a double. It has the same number of dots on both sides.

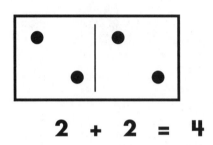

2 + 2 = 4

Look at each domino. Count the dots on each side. Write the number sentence.

_____ + _____ = 10

_____ + _____ = 8

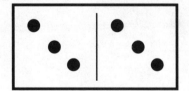

_____ + _____ = 6

_____ + _____ = 12

Under the Sea

Find the answers.

1.

3
+ 5
___

2.

5
+ 3
___

3.

7
+ 2
___

4.

2
+ 7
___

Power Practice

Look at the problems. The order of the numbers changed.
Did the answer change?

One More

Find the answers.

1. Kim has 3 balls.

Liza has 1 **more**.

Liza has _____  .

2. Suki has 5 [pencil] .

Abdul has 1 **more**.

Abdul has _____ [pencil] .

Draw the answer.

3. Kia has 4 [fish] .

Tori has 1 **more**.

Tori has _____ [fish] .

Use the blocks to count.

| 1 | 2 | 3 | 4 | 5 | 6 |

One Less

Find the answers.

1. Jill has 4 fish.

Sal has 1 **less**.

Sal has _____ .

2. Mel has 6 .

Ted has 1 **less**.

Ted has _____ .

Draw the answer.

3. Kit has 7 .

Lu has 1 **less**.

Lu has _____ .

Use the blocks to count.

1	2	3	4	5	6	7

Name _____

At the Pet Store

1. Cary has 5 . Mike has 4 . How many  **in all?**

a. Draw the fish. Count all the fish.

Cary   **Mike**

b. Write a number sentence: 5 + _____ = _____

2. Angela has 3 . Tara has 2 . How many  **in all?**

a. Start on 3. Count forward 2 blocks.

| 1 | 2 | 3 | 4 | 5 | 6 |

b. Write a number sentence. Show how many .

_____ + _____ = _____

Power Practice

 What math sign do you use to find how many in all?

Name _____

How Many Left?

1. Kessie has 6 . She finds homes for 3 .

a. How many  are **left**? _____

b. Write a number sentence.

_____ – _____ = _____

2. Dave has 8 . He gives away 3 .

a. Start at 8 on the number line. Count back 3 blocks.

1	2	3	4	5	6	7	8

Dave has _____  **left**.

b. Write a number sentence.

_____ – _____ = _____

Power Practice

 Think up a story to match this number sentence:

7 – 3 = _____ . Draw a picture of it on another sheet of paper.

Name _____

Opposite Problems

1.

Jared has 6 🍬. He gives away 2 🍬.

How many 🍬 does he have **left**? _____

2. Jared has 4 🍬. He gets 2 more 🍬.

a. Draw a picture.

b. How many 🍬 does he have **in all**? _____

More Opposite Problems

1. Corey has 9 ✏. She loses 4 ✏.

a. Draw a picture.

b. How many ✏ does Corey have **left**? _____

2. Corey has 5 ✏. She finds 4 more ✏.

a. Draw a picture.

b. How many ✏ does Corey have **in all**? _____

Power Practice

On another sheet of paper, write a story that matches each number sentence. Tell how the stories go together.

8 − 5 = _____.   3 + 5 = _____.

Make Your Own Problems

Make up a story for each problem. Draw a picture.

1.   4 + 4 = _____

2.   8 – 5 = _____

3.   3 + 7 = _____

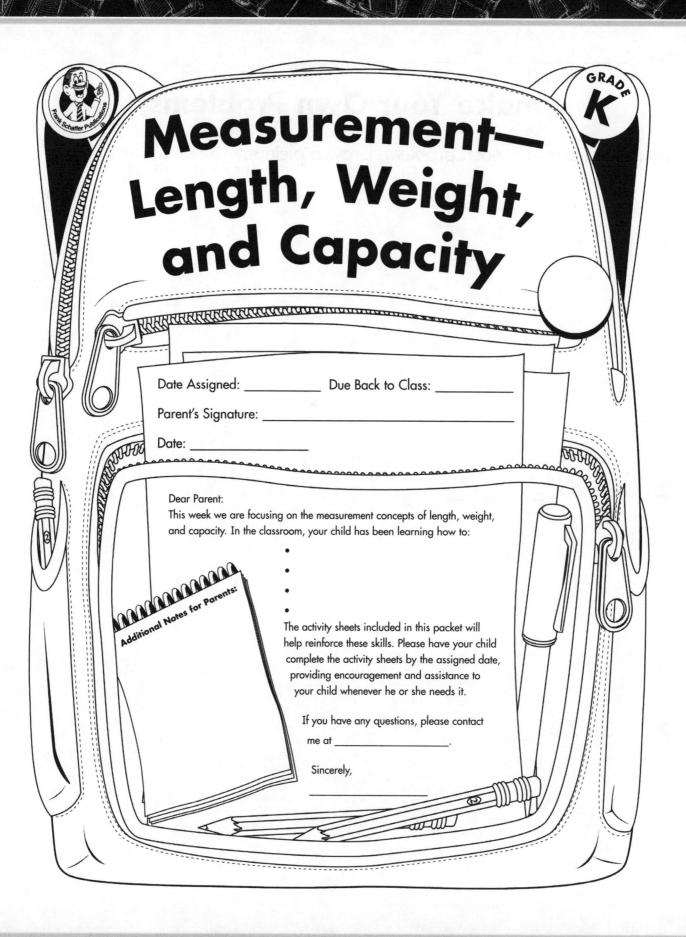

Measurement—Length, Weight, and Capacity

GRADE K

Date Assigned: _____ Due Back to Class: _____

Parent's Signature: _____

Date: _____

Additional Notes for Parents:

Dear Parent:
This week we are focusing on the measurement concepts of length, weight, and capacity. In the classroom, your child has been learning how to:

-
-
-

The activity sheets included in this packet will help reinforce these skills. Please have your child complete the activity sheets by the assigned date, providing encouragement and assistance to your child whenever he or she needs it.

If you have any questions, please contact me at _____.

Sincerely,

_____

How Do We Measure Length?

We measure things with a ruler. We can measure how long. **How long** means side to side.

Sometimes, we measure with pencils or paper clips. We also measure with rulers. We use inches and centimeters to tell how long.

1. How long means _____.

   a. side to side

   b. how thick

   c. how heavy

2. We measure with a _____.

3. We use _____ and _____ to tell how long.

   a. ounces and grams

   b. inches and centimeters

   c. gallons and liters

Paper Clip Measurement

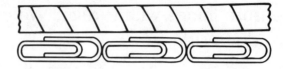

1 unit = 1 paper clip
The rope is 3 units long.

Write how many units.

1.

_____ units

2.

_____ units

3.
_____ units

4.

_____ units

5.

_____ units

Inching Along

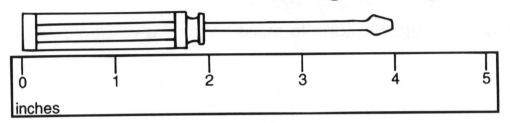

4 inches

Write how many inches.

1.

_____ inches

2.

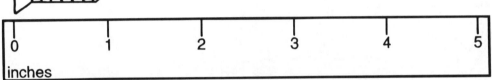

_____ inches

_____ inches

3.

_____ inches

4.

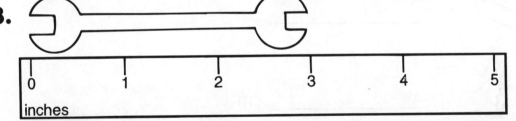

_____ inches

5.

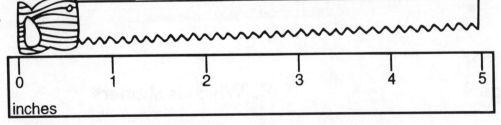

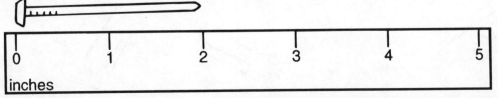

_____ inches

How Long?

Use a centimeter ruler or measuring tape to measure your own body.

1. leg _____ cm

2. finger _____ cm

3. hand _____ cm

4. foot _____ cm

5. forearm _____ cm

6. thumb _____ cm

Circle your answers.

7. Which is longer?

 or

8. Which is shorter?

 or

Name _____

Using a _____ Measuring Tape
(unit)

Measure things around your home. Write what you find.

I measured . . .	How long is it?

Name _____

Weigh Up

Look at each pair. Circle the **heavier** one.

1.

feather

chicken

2.

baby

doll

3.

pencil

crayons

4.

table

chair

 Math Power Packs: Reproducible Homework Packets *Grade K*

Which Holds More?

Circle which holds **more**.

1.

2.

3.

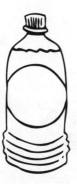 

4.

Holds More or Less

Circle which holds **less**.

1.

2.

3.

4.

Power Practice

Find two containers. Tell which one holds **more**. Write your answer.

Water Wash-Out

Answer the questions.

1. Rachelle was cleaning the bathroom. Circle which used **more** water.

5 cups   or   20 cups

2. A shower uses 40 liters of water. A bath uses 120 liters. You are trying to save water. Will you take a bath or shower?

_____

3. Joel is taking a bath.
He drops the soap. He spills 3 cups of water.
Then, he slips when getting out. He spills 5 cups of water.
How much does he spill **in all**?

$3 + 5 = $ _____

Check Your Skills

Find the answers.

1. How many 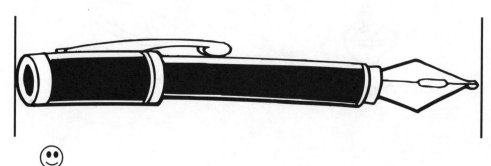 long is the pen? _____

2. Draw 3 . Follow the directions below.

Tall   **Taller**   **Tallest**

3. Which holds **more**?

4. Which is **heaviest**?

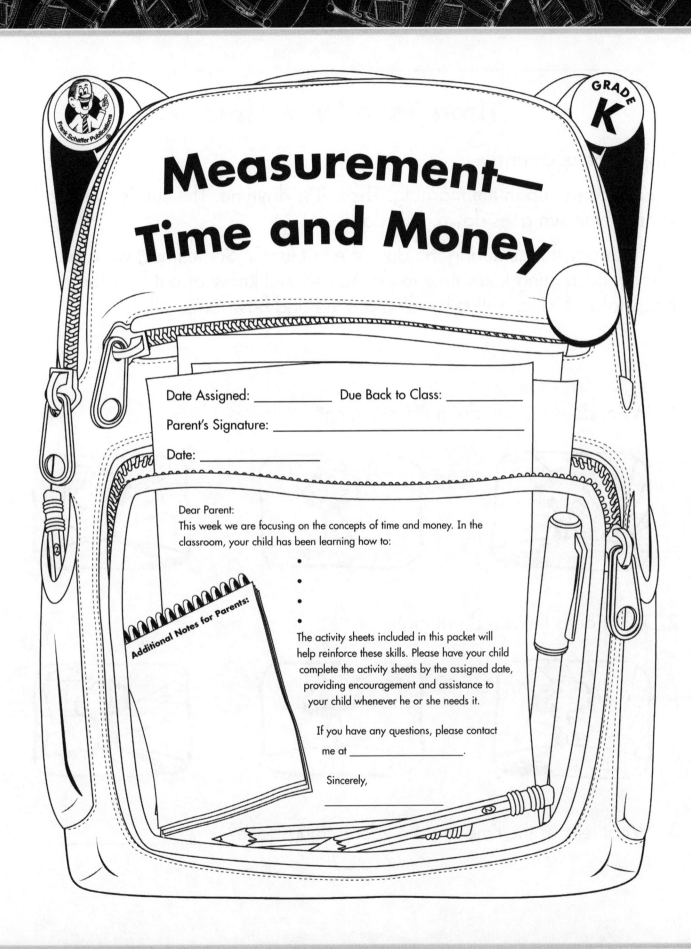

Measurement— Time and Money

GRADE K

Date Assigned: _____ Due Back to Class: _____

Parent's Signature: _____

Date: _____

Additional Notes for Parents:

Dear Parent:

This week we are focusing on the concepts of time and money. In the classroom, your child has been learning how to:

-
-
-
-

The activity sheets included in this packet will help reinforce these skills. Please have your child complete the activity sheets by the assigned date, providing encouragement and assistance to your child whenever he or she needs it.

If you have any questions, please contact me at _____.

Sincerely,

_____

Time Is All the Time

Answer the questions.

The sun comes up in the morning. Then, it is daytime. The sun is overhead. At night, the sun goes down. It is dark.

We do many things during the day. We eat lunch. Sometimes, we read a book. Each thing takes time to do. You should know about how long things take. A clock will tell you what time and how long.

1. What does the sun do in the morning?

2. What does the sun do at night?

3. What tells us the time and how long things take? _____

Time of the Day

Answer each question. Write the correct number on the line.

1   2   3

1. When do you [image] ? _____

2. When do you [image] ? _____

3. When do you [image] ? _____

Circle each picture that takes about one minute.

Name _____

One-Minute Marathon

In one minute, how many times can you . . .	Estimate	Count
Draw a square?		
Hop on one foot?		
Say "Rumpelstiltskin"?		
Clap your hands?		
Turn a circle?		
Say your name?		
Draw a circle?		

 Math Power Packs: Reproducible Homework Packets *Grade K*

Time

Circle the answers.

1. Which takes **more** time to get there?

2. Which takes **less** time to eat?

Power Practice

 Which takes the **most** time, brushing teeth, taking a bath, or washing your hands?

O'Clock

Write the time.

1. _____ o'clock

2. _____ o'clock

3. _____ o'clock

4. _____ o'clock

5. _____ o'clock

6. _____ o'clock

Power Practice

 Draw a clock. Show what time it is right now.

Digital Time

Write the time on the digital clock.

1.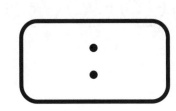

2.

3.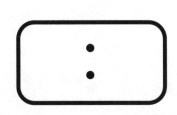

4.

5.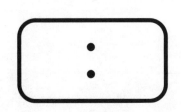

6.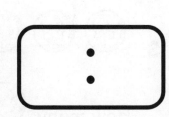

7.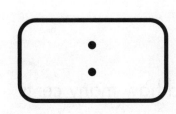

8.

Name _____

Counting Coins

Find the answers.

1.

How many 🪙 **in all?** _____

How many cents? _____

2.

How many 🪙 **in all?** _____

How many cents? _____

3.

How many 🪙 **in all?** _____

How many cents? _____

Power Practice

 How do you skip-count to find how many cents

for 🪙? For 🪙?

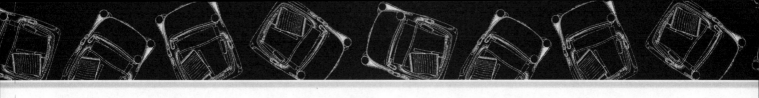

Name _____

Shopping

Draw a line to show what you can buy.

8¢

10¢

15¢

12¢

Power Practice

Which toy costs the **most**? Which toy costs the **least**?

How Much?

Draw the coins. Write the cost.

 costs 10¢.

1. How much do 5 cost? _____

2. How much do 7 cost? _____

3. How much do 10 cost? _____

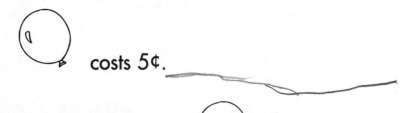 costs 5¢.

4. How much do 3 cost? _____

5. How much do 8 cost? _____

6. How much do 12 cost? _____

 Math Power Packs: Reproducible Homework Packets *Grade K*

Change Purse

Read each story. Find the number of coins. Use real coins to model the story if you like.

1.

I saved 2 pennies
every day for 3 days.
How many pennies
do I have **in all**?

_____

2.

I saved 2 dimes
every day for 4 days.
How many dimes do
I have **in all**?

_____

3.

I saved 3 nickels
every day for 3 days.
How many nickels do
I have **in all**?

_____

Power Practice

Find the number of coins in each problem if the coins were saved for one more day.

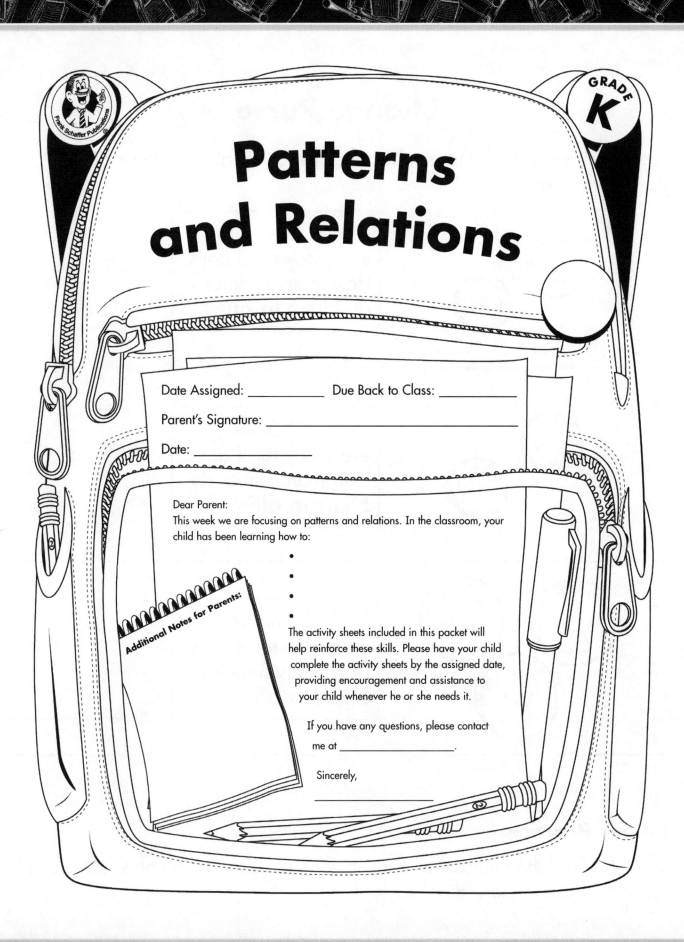

Patterns and Relations

Date Assigned: _____ Due Back to Class: _____

Parent's Signature: _____

Date: _____

Dear Parent:

This week we are focusing on patterns and relations. In the classroom, your child has been learning how to:

•

•

•

•

The activity sheets included in this packet will help reinforce these skills. Please have your child complete the activity sheets by the assigned date, providing encouragement and assistance to your child whenever he or she needs it.

If you have any questions, please contact me at _____.

Sincerely,

_____

Additional Notes for Parents:

Pretty Patterns

Read and answer the questions.

1. Cary was helping her mom. They were painting the bathroom. They were painting pictures. First, Mom painted a boat. Then, Cary painted a wave. Mom painted a boat again. Cary painted a wave again. Draw the pattern they painted.

2. Jermaine was putting tile in his shower. The tiles were different shapes. First, he put on a diamond. Next, he put on a circle. Finally, he put on a triangle. Draw the pattern he used.

3. Every morning, Tran did the same things. First, he took a shower. Next, he brushed his teeth. Then, he combed his hair. Tran followed this pattern each day. How many different parts are in Tran's pattern?

_____

Bathroom Patterns

Look at the bathroom. What patterns do you see?

Color the wallpaper pattern. Color with blue and yellow.

Color the floor pattern. Color with red, green, and orange.

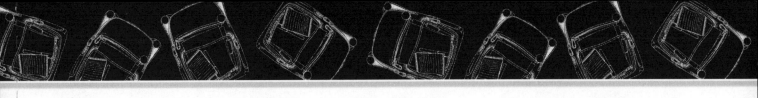

The Path to Treasure

This paper shows the secret pattern.
Find the path with the correct pattern.
Follow that path to the treasure.
Color the shapes in the correct path.

Power Practice

Look at each path again. What was the first shape in each path that did not follow the pattern? Circle those shapes.

Patterns

Name _____

Find the patterns.

1. Find the ★ pattern. Color the △ to match the pattern.

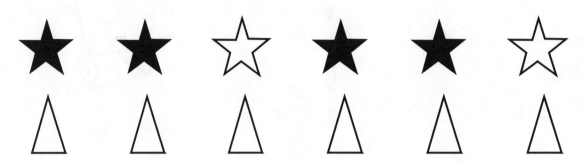

2. Find the 🌼 pattern. Draw 🙂 to match the pattern.

3. Make a sound pattern. Match the patterns above.
Use claps and stomps.

Power Practice

 What is the same about the patterns?
Write the pattern using **A** and **B**.

Math Power Packs: Reproducible Homework Packets *Grade K*

More Patterns

Find the patterns.

1. Find the 🍎 pattern. Color the 🍐 to match the pattern.

2. Find the 🔑 pattern. Draw shapes to match the pattern.

Use ◯ and ☐.

Power Practice

What is the same about the patterns?
Write the pattern using **A** and **B**.

Pattern Search

Find the patterns.

1. Find the 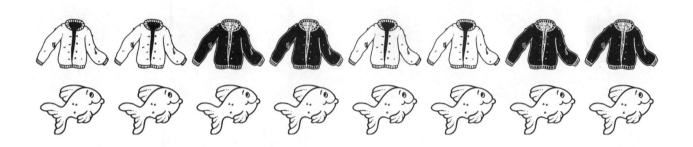 pattern. Color the fish to match the pattern.

2. Find the hat pattern. Draw ⭐ to match the pattern.

3. Make a sound pattern. Match the patterns above.
Use claps and stomps.

Power Practice

   What is the same about the patterns?
Write the pattern using **A** and **B**.

Name _____

Changing Things

Look at each set of pictures. They show things changing.
The pictures are in the wrong order. Show the right order.
Write the numbers **1**, **2**, **3**, and **4** by the pictures.

1.

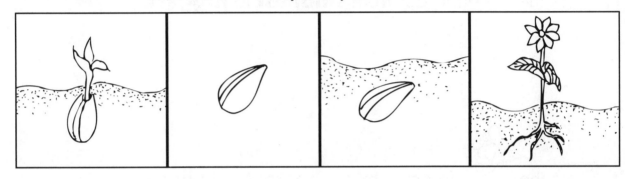

_____ _____ _____ _____

2.

_____ _____ _____ _____

3.

_____ _____ _____ _____

A Matter of Size

Cut out each group. Paste them on another sheet of paper.

1. Paste the 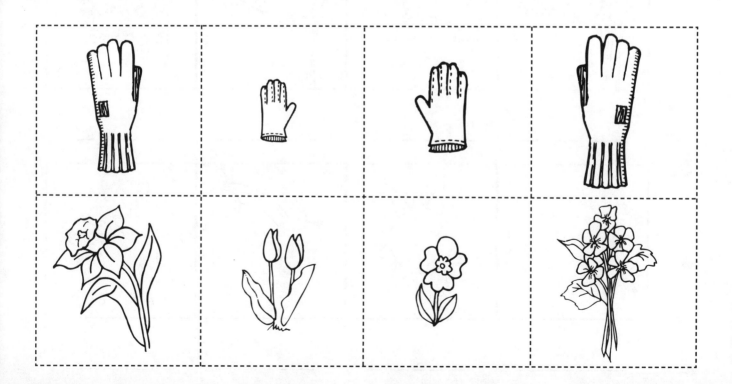 in order from **smallest** to **biggest**.

2. Paste the in order from **shortest** to **tallest**.

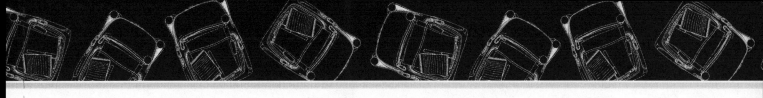

Name _____

What Does Not Belong?

Circle the one that **does not belong**. Name each set.

1.

Name: _____

2.

Name: _____

3.

Name: _____

Power Practice

 How do you find the one that **does not belong**?

Something's Different

Circle the one that **does not belong**. Name each set.

1.

Name: _____

2.

Name: _____

3.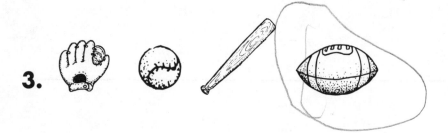

Name: _____

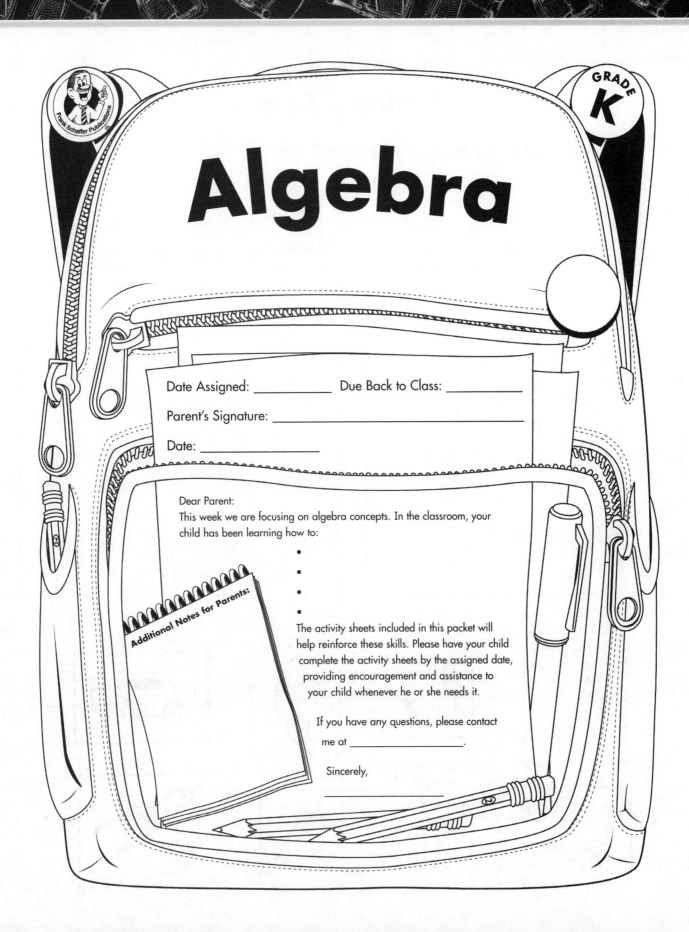

Algebra

GRADE K

Date Assigned: _____ Due Back to Class: _____

Parent's Signature: _____

Date: _____

Additional Notes for Parents:

Dear Parent:

This week we are focusing on algebra concepts. In the classroom, your child has been learning how to:

- •
- •
- •

The activity sheets included in this packet will help reinforce these skills. Please have your child complete the activity sheets by the assigned date, providing encouragement and assistance to your child whenever he or she needs it.

If you have any questions, please contact me at _____.

Sincerely,

_____

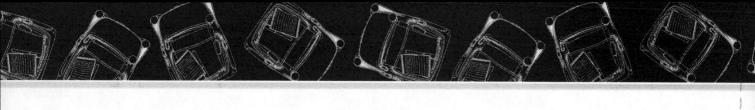

Making Sets

Cut out the pictures. Put the pictures into 2 sets.

Paste each set in a box. Name each set.

Name: _____   Name: _____

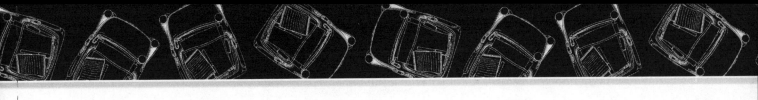

Name _____

Same and Different

Tell how the shapes in each group are alike. Tell how the shapes in each group are different from the shapes in the other groups. Draw a shape to match each shape in the group.

1.

2.

3.

Power Practice

Draw two more shapes that belong in each group.

Wonderful Wheels

Find the answers.

1. 1 + 3 = _____

2. 3 + 1 = _____

3. 4 + 2 = _____

4. 2 + 4 = _____

5. 3 + 4 = _____

6. 4 + 3 = _____

Power Practice

 Look at the problems. The order of the numbers changed.
Did the answer change?

Math Power Packs: Reproducible Homework Packets *Grade K*

Name _____

Number Construction

Find the answers.

1. Show 2 ways to write 6.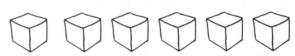

_____ + _____ = 6

_____ + _____ = 6

2. Show 2 ways to write 4.

_____ + _____ = 4

_____ + _____ = 4

3. 6 + 4 = _____

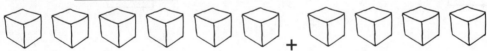

4. Show 2 ways to write 6 + 4 = _____.

_____ + _____ + 4 = _____

6 + _____ + _____ = _____

Power Practice

  Find a different way to write 10. Use 3 numbers. How did you do it?

Name _____

Guess the Number

What number goes in each empty box?

1. $11 + \boxed{} = 13$ **7.** $12 - \boxed{} = 10$

2. $6 + \boxed{} = 8$ **8.** $10 - \boxed{} = 8$

3. $5 + \boxed{} = 7$ **9.** $2 - \boxed{} = 0$

4. $4 + \boxed{} = 6$ **10.** $3 - \boxed{} = 1$

5. $1 + \boxed{} = 3$ **11.** $7 - \boxed{} = 5$

6. $9 + \boxed{} = 11$ **12.** $11 - \boxed{} = 9$

Power Practice

How are the problems the same? Write your answer.

What's Equal?

Match the **equal** things. Draw a line.

1. [four cubes]

A. 3 + 2

2. 3

B. [six cubes]

3. 4 + 6

C. 6 + 4

4. 2 + 4

D. 4

5. [five cubes]

E. 2 + 1

6. 8

F. 2 + 6

Power Practice

How do you decide if 2 things are **equal**? Write your answer.

How Many?

Find how many. Draw a model.

1.  on 4 ? _____

2. ears on 3  ? _____

3. on 2 ? _____

4. toes on 3 ? _____

Are There Enough?

Circle the correct answer.

1. 🦴 for 3 🐸 ?

🦴 🦴 🦴 🦴 🦴

🦴 🦴 🦴 🦴 🦴

😊   🙁

yes   no

---

2. 🛞 for 3 🏍 ?

🛞 🛞 🛞 🛞 🛞 🛞

😊   🙁

yes   no

---

3. 👢 for 4 🧒 ?

👢 👢 👢 👢

👢 👢 👢 👢

😊   🙁

yes   no

---

4. 🦴 for 2 🐕 ?

🦴 🦴 🦴 🦴

😊   🙁

yes   no

Check Your Skills

Find the answers.

1. Put these in order. Go from shortest to tallest. Write **1st**, **2nd**, and **3rd** on the lines.

_____   _____   _____

2. Circle what does not belong. Name the set.

Name: _____

3. Complete the pattern. Then, write the pattern using **A** and **B**.

More Check Your Skills

Find the answers.

1. Write the number 7 in 2 different ways.

_____ + _____ = 7

_____ + _____ = 7

2. Write the number 12 in 2 different ways.

_____ + _____ _____ = 12

_____ + _____ _____ = 12

3. How many legs on 3 ? _____

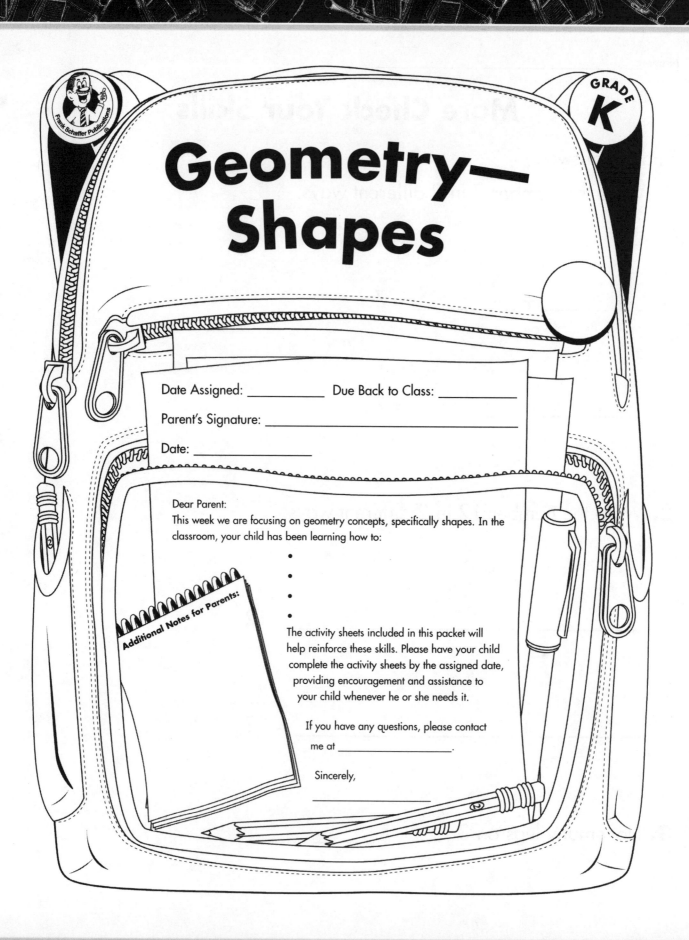

Geometry— Shapes

GRADE **K**

Date Assigned: _____ Due Back to Class: _____

Parent's Signature: _____

Date: _____

Additional Notes for Parents:

Dear Parent:

This week we are focusing on geometry concepts, specifically shapes. In the classroom, your child has been learning how to:

-
-
-
-

The activity sheets included in this packet will help reinforce these skills. Please have your child complete the activity sheets by the assigned date, providing encouragement and assistance to your child whenever he or she needs it.

If you have any questions, please contact me at _____.

Sincerely,

_____

Name _____

Slick Squares

Cut out the squares. Paste them in order from smallest to largest.

1st	2nd	3rd	4th

1. How many sides make 1 square? _____

2. How many sides make 2 squares? _____

3. How many sides make 3 squares? _____

4. How many sides make 4 squares? _____

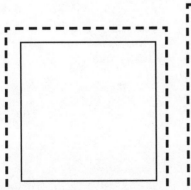 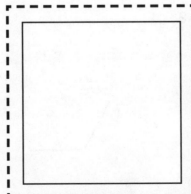 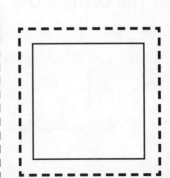 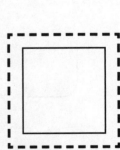

Name _____

Rowdy Rectangles

These are **rectangles**.

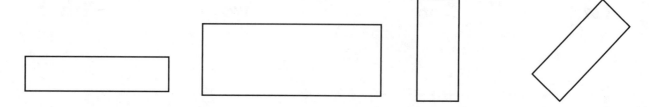

These are **not rectangles**.

1. How many sides on a rectangle? _____

2. Choose one. The sides are...?

3. How many corners on a rectangle? _____

4. Choose one. The corners are...?

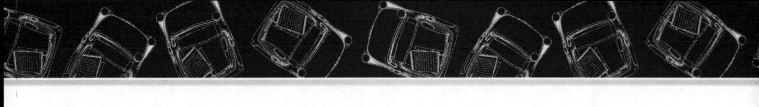

Name _____

More Rowdy Rectangles

Put an **x** in the box if the shape fits.
Decide if the shape is a rectangle.

	4 straight sides?	L-shaped corners?	Is it a rectangle?
1.			yes no
2.			yes no
3.			yes no
4.			yes no
5.			yes no
6.			yes no
7.			yes no
8.			yes no

Tricky Triangles

These are **triangles**.

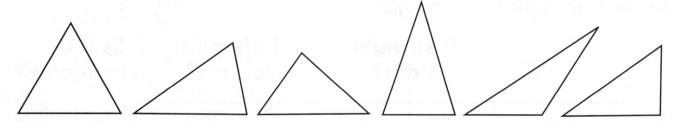

These are **not triangles**.

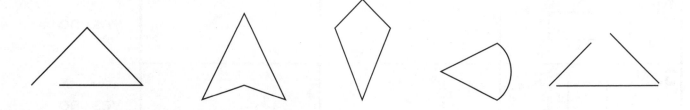

1. How many sides on a triangle? _____

2. What do the sides look like?

_____

3. How many corners on a triangle? _____

4. Circle the triangles.

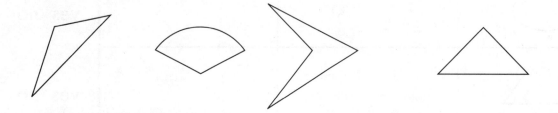

More Tricky Triangles

How many **triangles**? _____

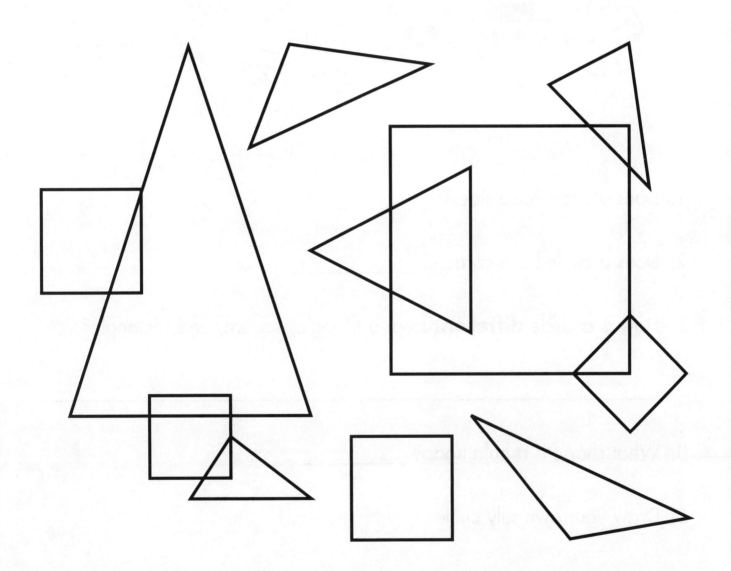

Name _____

Silly Circles

These shapes are **circles**.

1. Does a circle have sides? _____

2. Does a circle have corners? _____

3. How is a circle **different** from a triangle, square, and rectangle?

   _____

4. What shape is a hula hoop? _____

5. Draw your own silly circle.

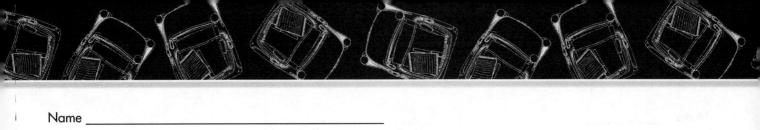

Sorting Shapes

Cut out the shapes. Paste the shapes into 2 sets. Name the sets.

Name: _____   Name: _____

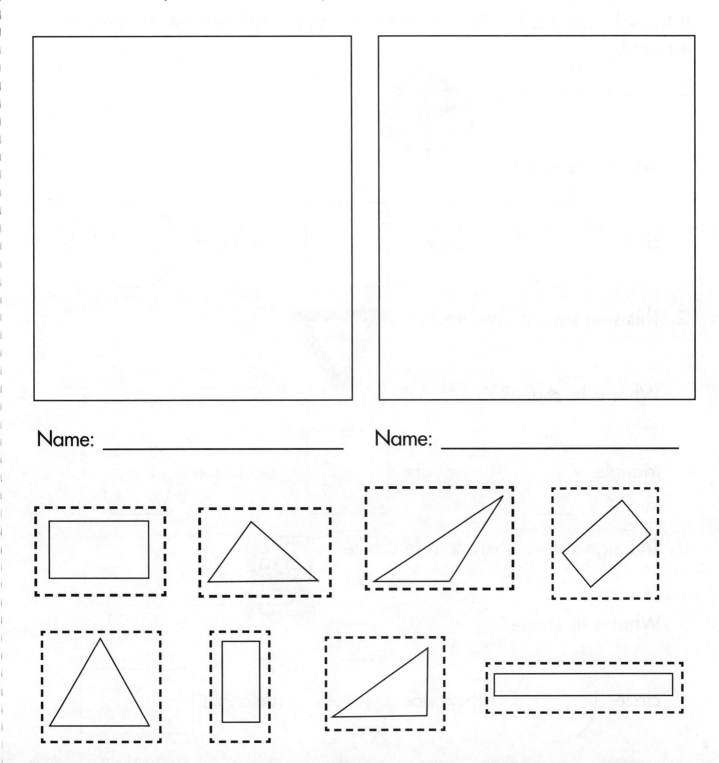

Sign Shapes

Circle the right answer.

A triangle has 3 sides. A rectangle has 4 sides. A circle has no sides. It is round.

1. This is a stop sign.

What is its shape?

circle 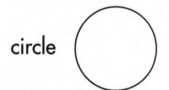   square   octagon

2. This sign says to slow down.

What is its shape?

triangle 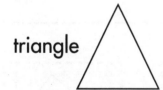   square   pentagon

3. This sign shows where to ride a bike.

What is its shape?

circle 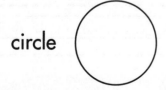   hexagon 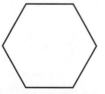   rectangle

Math Power Packs: Reproducible Homework Packets *Grade K*

Shapes Everywhere

Find the shapes.

Color the triangles green.

Color the squares red.

Color the rectangles blue.

Color the circles yellow.

Count the shapes. Write the number.

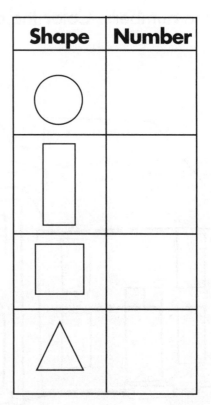

Shape	Number
⬤	
▭	
▢	
△	

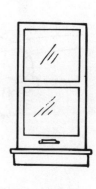

Power Practice

Find shapes around you. Where do you see the shapes? Write your answer.

Shapes in the Neighborhood

Count the shapes in the neighborhood.
Write the numbers. Color the picture.

1. How many ▭ ? _____

2. How many △ ? _____

3. How many ◯ ? _____

Data Analysis and Probability

GRADE K

Date Assigned: _____ Due Back to Class: _____

Parent's Signature: _____

Date: _____

Additional Notes for Parents:

Dear Parent:
This week we are focusing on data analysis and probability. In the classroom, your child has been learning how to:

-
-
-
-

The activity sheets included in this packet will help reinforce these skills. Please have your child complete the activity sheets by the assigned date, providing encouragement and assistance to your child whenever he or she needs it.

If you have any questions, please contact me at _____.

Sincerely,

_____

At the Grocery Store

Food Bought

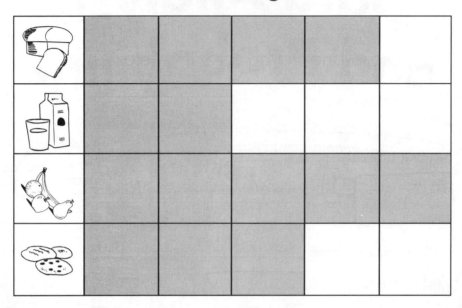

1. How many ? _____

2. How many ? _____

3. Which is **more**?

4. Which is **less**?

Name _____

Keeping Track of Things

Look at the graph.

It shows how many rainy days there were in March.

Rainy Days in March

Week 1	🌢🌢
Week 2	🌢🌢🌢
Week 3	🌢🌢
Week 4	🌢🌢🌢🌢

🌢 = 1 day

1. How much did it rain in week 4? _____

2. Which 2 weeks had the same number? _____

3. How many days of rain were there **in all**? _____

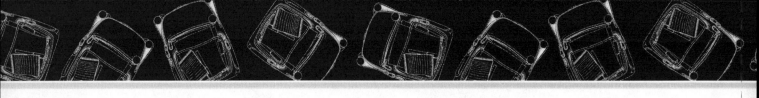

At the Watering Hole

Day 1	🐘 🐘
Day 2	🐘 🐘 🐘 🐘
Day 3	🐘 🐘 🐘 🐘 🐘 🐘
Day 4	🐘 🐘 🐘 🐘 🐘 🐘 🐘 🐘

1. The **most** 🐘 came on day _____ .

2. The **least** 🐘 came on day _____ .

3. How many 🐘 will come on day 5? _____
How do you know?

4. How many 🐘 will come on day 8? _____
How do you know?

Power Practice

The chart is called a **pictograph**.
What do you think "picto" stands for?

Tally Ho

Tally marks show how many.

1	2	3	4	5	6	7	8	9	10
I	II	III	IIII	⫟⫟⫟⫟⫟	⫟⫟⫟⫟⫟ I	⫟⫟⫟⫟⫟ II	⫟⫟⫟⫟⫟ III	⫟⫟⫟⫟⫟ IIII	⫟⫟⫟⫟⫟ ⫟⫟⫟⫟⫟

Count with tally marks.

1.

2.

Power Practice

 On another sheet of paper, use tally marks to count the girls in your class. Use tally marks to count the boys in your class. Which is more?

At the Zoo

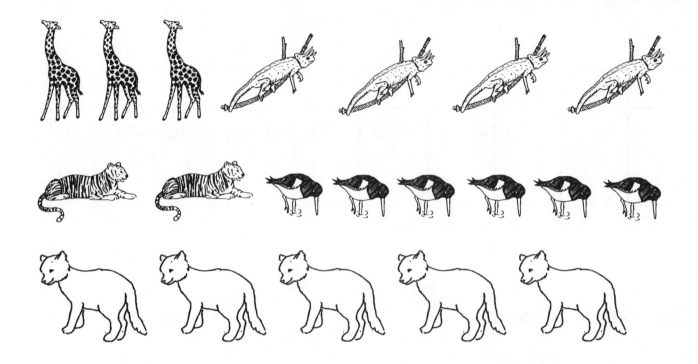

Make a tally table.

III				

Shape Sort

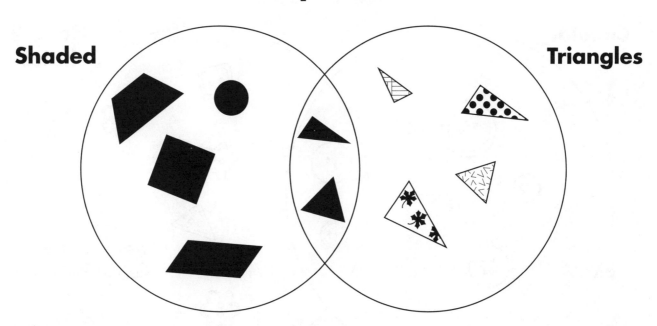

Shaded ... **Triangles**

1. How many shapes are shaded? _____

2. How many shapes are △? _____

3. How many △ are shaded? _____

Power Practice

How many shapes are in **both** circles?
Why are they in both circles?

Name _____

Button Sort

Circular

Have 2 holes

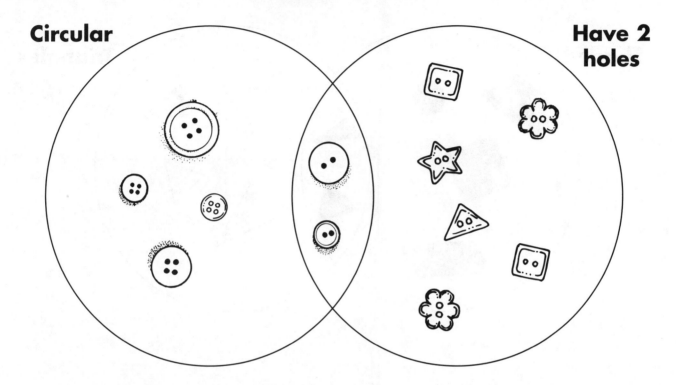

1. How many buttons are circles? _____

2. How many buttons have 2 holes? _____

3. How many buttons are circles with 2 holes? _____

Power Practice

How many buttons are in **both** circles?
Why are they in both circles?

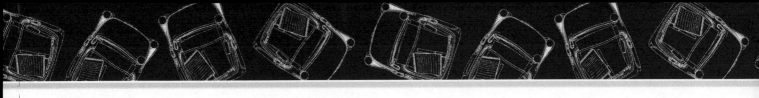

Check Your Skills

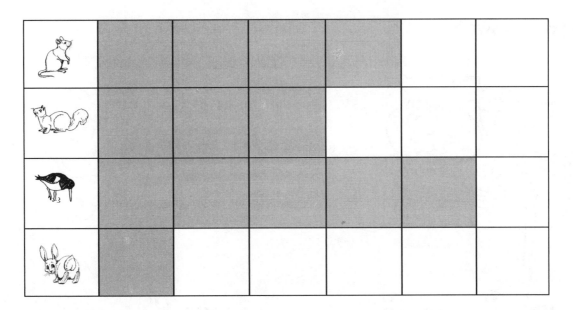

1. Make a tally table.

2. Which animals were seen the **most**?

3. Which animals were seen the **least**?

Is It Possible?

Circle your answer.

1.

yes 😊   no 🙁

2.

yes 😊   no 🙁

3.

yes   no 🙁

4.

yes   no 🙁

Is It Possible?

Circle your answer.

1.

yes 🙂   no ☹️

2.

yes 🙂   no ☹️

3.

yes 🙂   no ☹️

4.

yes 🙂   no ☹️

Problem Solving

Date Assigned: _____ Due Back to Class: _____

Parent's Signature: _____

Date: _____

Dear Parent:

This week we are focusing on problem solving. In the classroom, your child has been learning how to:

-
-
-
-

The activity sheets included in this packet will help reinforce these skills. Please have your child complete the activity sheets by the assigned date, providing encouragement and assistance to your child whenever he or she needs it.

If you have any questions, please contact me at _____.

Sincerely,

_____

Additional Notes for Parents:

Dudley Dragon

Draw Dudley's missing parts.

Dudley needs:

A pair of eyes

4 teeth

A pair of hands

8 tummy spots

A pair of ears

A pair of nose holes

10 whiskers

1 tail

Power Practice

 What is a **pair**?

A Number Poem

Find the answers.

Two drooling ,

Napping in the sun.

Along came 3 ,

Looking for some fun.

They spied 4 ,

Climbing up a tree,

Then saw 2 ,

Running around free.

1. How many and ?

2. Write a number sentence.
Show how many.

3. How many and ?

4. Write a number sentence.
Show how many.

5. How many animals **in all**?

6. Write a number sentence.
Show how many.

Power Practice

 What kind of math sign did you use?

Name _____

Birds and Bees

Finish the poem. Write a number sentence.

1. Four little black birds

    Sat in a tree.

    One flew away,

    Then there were _____.

    Number sentence: _____ − _____ = _____

2. Eight big yellow bees

    Land on a hive.

    Three bees flew away.

    Then there were _____.

    Number sentence: _____ − _____ = _____

3. Nine creepy spiders,

    Hang by the door.

    Five crawled away.

    Then there were _____.

    Number sentence: _____ − _____ = _____

Name _____

Count and Add

Answer the questions.

Draw pictures to help you.

1. Surya found 6 nails to make a birdhouse. Then, she found 4 nails. How many nails did she find **in all**?

_____

2. Bob's family has 1 car and 2 bikes. How many wheels do they have **in all**?

_____

3. Mary looked in the garage. She found 3 balls. She found 2 bats. She found 1 pair of skates. How many toys did she find **in all**?

_____

4. Jermaine's dad is fixing the car. He pulls off 3 screws and 4 caps. How many parts come out **in all**?

_____

The Long and Short of It

Follow the directions below.

1. Circle the **longest** .

2. Circle the **shortest** .

3. Circle the 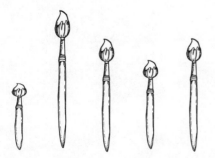 that are the **same** length.

Tall, Taller, Tallest

Follow the directions below.

1. Color the **tallest** brown.

2. Color the **shortest** yellow.

3. Color the other orange.

Buzzing Around

Circle where each bee flies.

Bee	Moves	Place
🐝	→ 2 ↓ 2	🏠 🌼 🌿
🐝	→ I ↓ I	🏠 🌼 🌿
🐝	← I ↓ 2	🏠 🌼 🌿
🐝	→ 3 ↑ 2	🏠 🌼 🌿

Power Practice

Draw an extra bee. Tell how to get from your bee to the hive.

Reading a Map

Look at the map.

Answer the questions.

Ling starts at her house.

1. Ling walks to the park to play hockey. She walks right _____ blocks. Then, she walks up 2 blocks

    a. 3   **b.** 4   **c.** 2

2. Ling walks to the grocery store. Then, she walks to school. How far does she walk in all?

    a. 5 blocks   **b.** 10 blocks   **c.** 7 blocks

3. On Monday, Ling and Jessie walk to school. They start at Jessie's house. They walk up 3 blocks. Then, they walk 1 block _____.

    a. right   **b.** left   **c.** down

Name _____

Problem-Solving Challenge

1. Put 7 paper clips into 2 sets. Make one set **more**. Make one set **less**. Draw the paper clips. Write a number sentence.

_____ + _____ = 7

2. 1 dog has a pair of ears.

2 dogs have _____ ears. 3 dogs have _____ ears.

3. Dana has 6 🍪🍪🍪🍪🍪🍪

She gave 2 away.

How many does she have **left**? _____

4. Laura picked 3 🌹.

She picked 4 🌷.

How many flowers did she pick **in all**? _____

Name _____

More Problem-Solving Challenge

1. Finish the pattern. Then, write the pattern using **A** and **B**.

2. Draw a rectangle.

How many sides? _____

How many corners? _____

3. Circle the **tallest** tree.

4. Circle the amount that is **more**.

Answer Key

Match and Paste . . . . **Page 10**

How Many Dots? . . . . **Page 11**
Answers will vary.

Wally Worm . . . . **Page 12**
 1. 1
 2. 20
 3. 8
 4. 12
 5. 9
 6. 16
Power Practice: Students should write numbers 20, 19, 18, 17, etc.

On the Farm . . . . **Page 13**
 1. ducks
 2. cows
 3. ducks

Seeing Spots . . . . **Page 14**
 1. no
 2. yes
 3. yes
 4. yes
 5. no
Power Practice: Students should explain that they counted to find the correct answers.

Something's Fishy . . . . **Page 15**
Check students' coloring.

Who Has More? . . . . **Page 16**
 1. Joe
 2. Jada
 3. Juan
 4. Jae
 5. Tom
 6. Carl
Power Practice: Students should explain the word **more** to a family member.

Who Has Less? . . . . **Page 17**
 1. Brent
 2. Shaun
 3. Evita
 4. Lili
 5. Meg
 6. Mark
Power Practice: Students should explain the word **less** to a family member.

Show What You Know . . . . **Page 18**
Answers will vary. Check students' drawings.

In What Order? . . . . **Page 19**
Check matching.
Power Practice: All the places behind the penguin move up 1.

Number Walk . . . . **Page 22**
Power Practice: 20; 21

Answer Key

Count the Animals . . . . **Page 23**
horse—2
cow—3
chicken—4
pig—3
goat—2
dog—1
sheep—1
duck—2
Power Practice: chickens

Count How Many . . . . **Page 24**

2
6
5
4
3
7

Count the Dots . . . . **Page 25**

7   3
2   10
8   1
0   4
2   6

Tool Time . . . . **Page 26**
1. 9
2. 12
3. 8
4. 7

Picnic Time . . . . **Page 27**
1. 4
2. 3
3. 7
4. 2
5. 1
6. 3
7. 10
8. 7 + 3 = 10

At the Game . . . . **Page 28**
1. 2
2. 3
3. 5
4. 2 + 3 = 5
Power Practice: +

Count and Tally . . . . **Page 29**
dragonflies—6 tally marks
frogs—9 tally marks
butterflies—5 tally marks

How Many Are Left? . . . . **Page 30**
1. 8
3. 5
4. 3
5. 10
7. 6
8. 4
Power Practice: subtract

Fill in the Boxes . . . . **Page 32**
1. 1 + 1 = 2
2. 2 + 2 = 4
3. 2 + 4 = 6
4. 4 + 4 = 8

Answer Key

Double Dominoes . . . . **Page 33**
5 + 5 = 10
4 + 4 = 8
3 + 3 = 6
6 + 6 = 12

Under the Sea . . . . **Page 34**
 1. 8
 2. 8
 3. 9
 4. 9
Power Practice: When the numbers switched places, the answer was still the same.

One More . . . . **Page 35**
 1. 4
 2. 6
 3. 5

One Less . . . . **Page 36**
 1. 3
 2. 5
 3. 6

At the Pet Store . . . . **Page 37**
 1. a. Check drawings.
   b. 5 + 4 = 9
 2. a. 5
   b. 3 + 2 = 5
Power Practice: +

How Many Left? . . . . **Page 38**
 1. a. 3
   b. 6 − 3 = 3
 2. a. 5
   b. 8 − 3 = 5
Power Practice: Stories and drawings will vary.

Opposite Problems . . . . **Page 39**
 1. 4
 2. b. 6

More Opposite Problems . . . . . . **Page 40**
 1. b. 5
 2. b. 9
Power Practice: Stories will vary.

Make Your Own Problems . . . . . **Page 41**
Answers will vary.

How Do We Measure Length? . . . **Page 43**
 1. a
 2. ruler
 3. b

Paper Clip Measurement . . . . . . **Page 44**
 1. 5 units
 2. 3 units
 3. 2 units
 4. 6 units
 5. 4 units

Inching Along . . . . **Page 45**
 1. 1 inch
 2. 4 inches
 3. 3 inches
 4. 5 inches
 5. 2 inches

How Long? . . . . **Page 46**
Answers will vary.

Using a Measuring Tape . . . . . . **Page 47**
Answers will vary.

Answer Key

Weigh Up . . . . **Page 48**
1. chicken
2. baby
3. crayons
4. table

Which Holds More? . . . . **Page 49**
1. jug
2. large carton
3. soda bottle
4. water bottle

Holds More or Less . . . . **Page 50**
1. first
2. second
3. second
4. first
Power Practice: Answers will vary.

Water Wash-Out . . . . **Page 51**
1. bath
2. shower
3. 8 cups

Check Your Skills . . . . **Page 52**
1. 4 paper clips (using a 3 cm paper clip)
2. Check students' drawings.
3. gallon milk jug
4. watermelon

Time Is All the Time . . . . **Page 54**
1. it comes up
2. it goes down
3. clock

Time of the Day . . . . **Page 55**
1. 3
2. 1
3. 2
Circled: blowing bubble, feeding dog

One-Minute Marathon . . . . **Page 56**
Answers will vary.

Time . . . . **Page 57**
1. walking
2. small sandwich
Power Practice: taking a bath

O'Clock . . . . **Page 58**
1. 3 o'clock
2. 10 o'clock
3. 9 o'clock
4. 6 o'clock
5. 5 o'clock
6. 7 o'clock
Power Practice: Answers will vary.

Digital Time . . . . **Page 59**
1. 3:00
2. 8:00
3. 2:00
4. 11:00
5. 6:00
6. 5:00
7. 9:00
8. 4:00

Answer Key

Counting Coins . . . . **Page 60**
1. 10 pennies; 10 cents
2. 3 nickels; 15 cents
3. 4 dimes; 40 cents
Power Practice: Skip-count by 5's to find how many cents for nickels. Skip-count by 10's to find how many cents for dimes.

Shopping . . . . **Page 61**
3 pennies and a nickel = 8 ¢, doll
2 pennies and 2 nickels = 12 ¢, ball
5 pennies and a nickel = 10 ¢, boat
5 pennies and 2 nickels = 15 ¢, airplane
Power Practice: The airplane costs the most. The doll costs the least.

How Much? . . . . **Page 62**
1. 50¢
2. 70¢
3. $1.00
4. 15¢
5. 40¢
6. 60¢

Change Purse . . . . **Page 63**
1. 6
2. 8
3. 9
Power Practice: 8, 10, 12

Pretty Patterns . . . . **Page 65**
1. boat, wave
2. diamond, circle, triangle
3. 3 parts

Bathroom Patterns . . . . **Page 66**
Wallpaper should be colored in blue/yellow pattern. Floor should be colored in a red/green/orange pattern.

The Path to Treasure . . . . **Page 67**
The path that leads to the treasure is: heart, heart, star, heart, heart, star, heart, heart, star. Power Practice: In the first path, the first star should be circled. In the second path, the second star should be circled.

Patterns . . . . **Page 68**
1. Color 2 triangles, leave 1 white (repeat)
2. 2 big smiley faces, 1 small smiley face (repeat)
3. clap, clap, stomp, clap, clap, stomp
Power Practice: AABAAB

More Patterns . . . . **Page 69**
1. 1 dark, 1 white (repeat)
2. circle, square, circle, square, circle, square
Power Practice: ABABAB

Pattern Search . . . . **Page 70**
1. 2 white, 2 dark (repeat)
2. 2 small stars, 2 large stars (repeat)
3. clap, clap, stomp, stomp (repeat)
Power Practice: AABBAABB

Changing Things . . . . **Page 71**
1. 3, 1, 2, 4
2. 2, 1, 3, 4
3. 1, 3, 4, 2

A Matter of Size . . . . **Page 72**
Check order.

Answer Key

What Does Not Belong? . . . . . . **Page 73**
1. ant; insects with wings
2. carrot; fruit
3. fork; things you write with
Power Practice: Find what most of the things have in common. Determine what's different.

Something's Different . . . . **Page 74**
1. feather; plants
2. snake; animals with legs
3. football; things used in baseball

Making Sets . . . . **Page 76**
Students could split the objects into toys and tools.

Same and Different . . . . **Page 77**
1. one or more similarly rounded shapes
2. one or more shapes with four sides and four corners
3. one or more triangles
Power Practice: Check drawings.

Wonderful Wheels . . . . **Page 78**
1. 4
2. 4
3. 6
4. 6
5. 7
6. 7
Power Practice: When the numbers switched places, the answer was still the same.

Number Construction . . . . **Page 79**
Answers may vary.
1. $1 + 5 = 6$; $3 + 3 = 6$; $2 + 4 = 6$
2. $1 + 3 = 4$; $2 + 2 = 4$
3. $6 + 4 = 10$
4. $5 + 1 + 4 = 10$ or $3 + 3 + 4 = 10$ or $2 + 4 + 4 = 10$
$6 + 1 + 3 = 10$ or $6 + 2 + 2 = 10$
Power Practice: Answers will vary.

Guess the Number . . . . **Page 80**
1–12. 2
Power Practice: The first 6 problems all add 2. Problems **7–12** all subtract 2.

What's Equal? . . . . **Page 81**
1. D
2. E
3. C
4. B
5. A
6. F
Power Practice: They have the same value.

How Many? . . . . **Page 82**
1. 8
2. 6
3. 8
4. 15

Are There Enough? . . . . **Page 83**
1. no; 12 legs would be needed
2. yes
3. yes
4. no; 8 legs would be needed

Answer Key

Check Your Skills . . . . **Page 84**
1. 2nd, 1st, 3rd
2. fox; animals usually found in water
3. ABBABB

More Check Your Skills . . . . **Page 85**
1. Answers will vary. Check arithmetic.
2. Answers will vary. Check arithmetic.
3. 12

Slick Squares . . . . **Page 87**
Check size order of squares.
1. 4
2. 8
3. 12
4. 16

Rowdy Rectangles . . . . **Page 88**
1. 4
2. straight
3. 4
4. L-shaped

More Rowdy Rectangles . . . . . . **Page 89**
1. no (doesn't have L-shaped corners)
2. yes
3. yes
4. no (doesn't have L-shaped corners)
5. no (sides aren't straight)
6. yes
7. no (sides aren't straight)
8. no (doesn't have L-shaped corners)

Tricky Triangles . . . . **Page 90**
1. 3
2. straight lines
3. 3
4. 2 triangles

More Tricky Triangles . . . . **Page 91**
There are 11 different triangles.

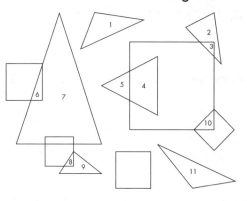

Silly Circles . . . . **Page 92**
1. no
2. no
3. Triangles, squares, and rectangles all have straight sides and corners. A circle doesn't have either.
4. circle
5. Drawings will vary.

Sorting Shapes . . . . **Page 93**
Shapes should be sorted into rectangles and triangles.

Sign Shapes . . . . **Page 94**
1. octagon
2. triangle
3. rectangle

Shapes Everywhere . . . . **Page 95**
4 circles; button, top of stool, 2 wagon wheels
9 rectangles; bottom and 4 sides of wagon, 2 window panes, window frame, window ledge
12 squares; 9 on cubes, 3 on jack-in-the-box
6 triangles; 2 on jack-in-the-box, 4 on pyramid
Power Practice: Answers will vary.

Answer Key

Shapes in the Neighborhood . . . Page 96
Numbers are approximate:
58 rectangles, 17 triangles,
8 circles

At the Grocery Store . . . . Page 98
1. 2
2. 4
3. fruit
4. milk

Keeping Track of Things . . . . Page 99
1. 4 days
2. 1 and 3
3. 11 days

At the Watering Hole . . . . Page 100
1. 4
2. 1
3. 10; 2 more elephants each day
4. 16; extend table, skip-count by 2's
Power Practice: "Picto" stands for picture. Each picture represents 1 elephant.

Tally Ho . . . . Page 101
1. ⅢⅡ 2. ⅠⅠⅠⅠ
Power Practice: Answers should reflect
your classroom.

At the Zoo . . . . Page 102
Check tally marks.
3 giraffes; 4 chameleons; 2 tigers; 6 birds; 5 foxes

Shape Sort . . . . Page 103
1. 6
2. 6
3. 2
Power Practice: 2; They are triangles, and they are shaded.

Button Sort . . . . Page 104
1. 6
2. 8
3. 2
Power Practice: 2; These buttons are circles; and they have 2 holes.

Check Your Skills . . . . Page 105
1. 4 mice, 3 squirrels, 5 birds, 1 rabbit
2. birds
3. rabbits

Is It Possible? . . . . Page 106
1. yes
2. no
3. no
4. yes

Is It Possible? . . . . Page 107
1. no
2. yes or no (some cultures eat bugs)
3. yes
4. no

Dudley Dragon . . . . Page 109
Check number of each missing part drawn.
Power Practice: A group of two

A Number Poem . . . . Page 110
1. 5
2. 2 + 3 = 5
3. 6
4. 4 + 2 = 6
5. 11
6. 5 + 6 = 11
Power Practice: +

Answer Key

Birds and Bees . . . . **Page 111**
 1. 3; 4–1= 3
 2. 5; 8–3= 5
 3. 4; 9–5= 4

Count and Add . . . . **Page 112**
 1. 10 nails
 2. 8 wheels
 3. 6 toys
 4. 7 parts

The Long and Short of It . . . . . **Page 113**
 1. first pencil
 2. middle tree
 3. third and fifth brush

Tall, Taller, Tallest . . . . **Page 114**
1st: brown
2nd: yellow
3rd: orange

Buzzing Around . . . . **Page 115**

Power Practice: Answers will vary.

Reading a Map . . . . **Page 116**
 1. c
 2. a
 3. b

Problem-Solving Challenge . . . **Page 117**
 1. Check to make sure numbers add up to 7.
 2. 4; 6
 3. 4
 4. 7

More Problem-Solving Challenge . **Page 118**
 1. AABAABAAB
 2. Check rectangle; 4 sides; 4 corners
 3. Make sure tallest tree is circled.
 4. 6 should be circled

Notes